Photography by Unearthed Photographical

Dr. Kaufman Walker was born in Kitchener, Ontario, Canada, and moved to Alexandria, Virginia, as a child. She attended TC Williams High School and received a Bachelor of Science in Psychology at Lynchburg College (now The University of Lynchburg), a Master of Arts in Community Counseling at Marymount University, and her PhD in Counseling with an emphasis in trauma, crisis, and substance use from George Washington University. Dr. Kaufman Walker is a licensed counselor in Virginia, West Virginia, DC, Maryland, and Florida. She works with children and adults and specializes in trauma, crisis, and grief and loss in Middleburg, Virginia. She currently lives in Bluemont, VA, on Chance Farm with her husband, two children, and a menagerie of animal friends. She found inspiration to write *What Is Family?* through her experiences with children in foster care and the dearth of resources discussing the concept of family. Her vision materialized when she welcomed Bubs, an orphaned deer, into her home, nurturing her until she was prepared to venture out on her own.

Dr. Jennifer Elizabeth Kaufman Walker
Illustrated by Alexandra Birchmore

WHAT IS FAMILY?

The Story of Bubs

AUSTIN MACAULEY PUBLISHERS™

LONDON • CAMBRIDGE • NEW YORK • SHARJAH

Ordering Information
Quantity sales: Special discounts are available on quantity purchases by corporations, associations, and others. For details, contact the publisher at the address below.

Publisher's Cataloging-in-Publication data
Walker, Dr. Jennifer Elizabeth Kaufman.
What Is Family?

ISBN 9798891556751 (Paperback)
ISBN 9798891556768 (Hardback)
ISBN 9798891556775 (ePub e-book)

Library of Congress Control Number: 2024914134

www.austinmacauley.com/us

First Published 2024
Austin Macauley Publishers LLC
40 Wall Street, 33rd Floor, Suite 3302
New York, NY 10005
USA

mail-usa@austinmacauley.com
+1 (646) 5125767

I dedicate this book to my parents, Karen and Rob Kaufman; my uncle, Bob Chapeskie; my husband, Ryan Walker; and my children, Josephine and Gunnar Walker. Thank you for always believing in me and cheering me on along the way. I love you all to the moon and across every star.

A special thanks to all the people who helped raise the real-life Bubs: Robyn Anderson, Erin Green, and Harrison Young. I love and appreciate all of you more than you know.

About the Illustrator: Alexandra Birchmore

Alexandra is an artist from a small town in the Cotswolds, England. She started her art career in CGI but having always drawn and painted animals from a young age, she eventually transitioned into traditionally painting pets and animals—painting and animals being two of her great loves. Alexandra finds inspiration from the rolling hills and woodlands around her town, and she aims to capture the life and spirit of every creature she gets the chance to paint.

Bubs woke to the bright morning sun. It was such a beautiful day, but she realized she was feeling lonely, as she did not have a family. As she lay there, looking at her reflection in the pond, she wondered, "What is a family?" Determined to find the answer to that very question, she decided to ask her friends.

Suddenly, Bub's friend, Mr. Frog, popped his head out of the water. Mr. Frog was always around, checking on Bubs to make sure she was doing okay. Bubs knew that Mr. Frog loved her and accepted her, which made Bubs feel safe and protected.

"Mr. Frog, is family someone who looks like me?" Bubs asked.

The frog immediately responded, "Ribbet...why no, Bubs, family is someone you love who loves you exactly the way you are. A family member's love is unconditional, meaning you know no matter what happens, they will always love you."

Confused, Bubs continued her quest. She walked along the fence line and saw her friend, Ms. Turtle, sauntering towards another pond. Bubs knew Ms. Turtle was very busy, but regardless of her schedule, Ms. Turtle always made time for Bubs, often coming to sit with her.

"Excuse me, Ms. Turtle, do you know what a family is?"

Ms. Turtle looked up and said, "Well, I believe a family is caring and making you a priority. Family is made up of those who not only care about you but also make time for you," and then slowly moved off.

Poor Bubs was truly baffled but remained determined to find the answer she yearned for. As she walked into the field, Bubs saw her good friend, Mr. Eagle, soaring nearby. With a graceful swoop, Mr. Eagle descended and landed close by. Bubs ran as fast as she could to ask the eagle if he understood the meaning of family. Bubs knew that Mr. Eagle would be excited about her quest, as he never failed to support and cheer Bubs on.

"Hi, my eagle friend, I was wondering if you could tell me what family is!"

The eagle looked right at Bubs and replied in a stern voice, "Family are those who are your biggest cheerleaders! They want what is best for you and support you even when they may not fully agree with your decisions or behaviors." Bubs thanked Mr. Eagle as he flew off into the sky.

Bubs paused for a moment, pondering what the eagle had said...

Hmm, cheer me on and want what is best for me?

Undeterred, Bubs continued through the field and into the woods. As Bubs entered the forest, she saw Mrs. Squirrel and decided to ask if she knew the answer. Bubs loved Mrs. Squirrel, because Bubs knew she could trust her.

"Hi there, Mrs. Squirrel! Do you know what family is?"

Mrs. Squirrel continued sniffing the ground, then suddenly paused and said, "Family means that you can trust what they tell you and that they will keep their word to you no matter what."

"Oh, like I feel about you, Mrs. Squirrel?" Bubs asked.

"I sure hope that is how I make you feel, Bubs." Mrs. Squirrel responded as she scurried off into the leaves.

As Bubs took a moment to ponder what Mrs. Squirrel had said, she smiled, thinking about how she could come to Mrs. Squirrel with her thoughts and feelings, knowing that she could trust her to be honest and stand by her word.

Bubs realized it was getting late; she needed to hurry if she wanted to find the answer to her question. Just then, she heard something scurrying on the ground. Looking down, she saw a mouse among the leaves. It was Mr. Mouse! Bubs always came to Mr. Mouse for his sage advice because he was honest, kind, and thoughtful, never leading her astray. Excitedly, Bubs thought that Mr. Mouse would surely know the answer to her question!

"Pardon me, Mr. Mouse, I have been trying to figure out exactly what family is all about! But no one has been able to answer my question. I have been told that family is someone who checks on you, loves you unconditionally, makes you a priority, cheers you on, and supports you—someone you can trust, who keeps their word, and makes you feel safe and protected. Do you think you have the answer?"

Mr. Mouse looked straight at Bubs and said, "Family is many things, my little friend. In fact, family is all those things — it is unconditional love, consideration, support, feeling heard, understood, safe, and protected. Family is not always someone who looks like you; in fact, sometimes family are those you choose!"

Bubs looked at Mr. Mouse, completely perplexed. "I do not understand, Mouse, will you please explain?"

"If you are very lucky, you will find that family is made up of those who love you, those that you know will always be there and that you can trust. They make you feel safe and protected and a priority while cheering you on along the way. Family takes the time to listen to what you have to say, and even if they may not completely understand how you are feeling, they will respond in ways that leave you feeling supported and heard. Most importantly, family does not always look like you. It is the inside that counts, the love that others hold in their hearts just for you. Family makes one's life better by just being a part of it."

Bubs thought about what the Mouse said and asked, "So are you part of my family, Mr. Mouse? You take the time to talk with me without judgment and give me thoughtful advice."
Mr. Mouse responded, "Why, yes, my sweet Bubs, I am a part of your family, as is Ms. Turtle, Mr. Frog, Mrs. Squirrel, and Mr. Eagle."

Bubs thanked Mr. Mouse and walked away, smiling. Bubs found her answer! Family was not about sharing what is on the outside but instead; family is made up of those who look alike on the inside! They are those who reflect the same love in their hearts for you as you do for them. Family is being connected to those who you hold dear; to be a part of something that makes you feel stronger and protected, cared for, and supported all at once.

As Bubs curled up in the grass to settle in for the night, she felt at peace knowing that her family was surrounding her as she slept. It was Mr. Eagle cheering her on and wanting what was best for Bubs. It was Mrs. Squirrel who Bubs could be honest with and trust, Mr. Mouse who was kind and thoughtful, and who Bubs went to for advice. It was Ms. Turtle, who checked on Bubs and made her feel like a priority, and Mr. Frog, who made Bubs feel safe and loved by taking the time to make sure she was okay. For the first time in a long time, Bubs drifted off to sleep feeling safe and loved, knowing that she would always have her chosen family right beside her.

THE END

Printed in the USA
CPSIA information can be obtained
at www.ICGtesting.com
CBHW041958130924

14158CB00017B/290

* 9 7 9 8 8 9 1 5 5 6 7 6 8 *